Dissolve

A collection of reflective poetry

Nistha Ghosh

BookLeaf Publishing

India | USA | UK

Made with ❤ on the BookLeaf Publishing Platform
www.bookleafpub.in
www.bookleafpub.com

Dedication

To all seekers, who are willing to lose it all, for nothing.

Preface

Poems are expression of words
That often go unspoken
Words are expression of feelings
That are often kept hidden.

To a young adolescent girl, poetry offered an escape from reality. Life was gracious enough to provide a comfortable survival but something deep within me was always longing to go beyond my capacities. A heart that had always found warmth and fulfilment in the lap of nature was now feeling a strange growing void. The mind was asking for deeper satisfaction of life. At the same time society started imposing its virtuous ways for a good young woman. Unable to comprehend the confusion within myself, and in the chaos of how I am supposed to be, a deep longing grew to escape the reality. In those moments, poetry gave me the space to pour my heart out where I could set myself free. During the dark hours of the night, when the visual stimulations are low and imagination is high, I would spread my invisible wings and fly beyond the limits of the sky.

But with growing years the void deepened and the longing for fulfilment intensified. Without any guidance or knowledge, I was frantically searching for it outside- in nature, relationships, love, sacrifice and God- but couldn't find it. As the seeking became stronger, I turned inwards and started searching within myself. Instead of answers, I stumbled upon a much deeper question- Who am I? Now this longing to know surfaced my search for my identity, purpose, existence and the truth of life. As these questions gained clarity, my experience of myself started transforming. When the seeking gained sheer intensity, my Guru graced with his presence and offered tools to deepen this search for truth. My seeking got spiritual direction and effortlessly flowed in joy, bliss, peace and fulfilment. There is no more a need to escape the reality as my experience of life has transcended the physicality of body, mind and emotions. This journey has broadened with deeper experiences where life often explodes to new dimensions of truth and existence. This quest of seeking is not yet over but now it resonates with life in its true state. Life has dropped its needless meanings and is in tune with the truth.

This book is a collection of my poems written through a span of over a decade. Each piece captures a fragment of my personal experience which offers a glimpse into my journey. The cover of this book is designed incorporating one of my own painting "wildflowers". Wildflowers are the touch of the divine in the ordinary. As you read through these poems of seeking, I hope you keep an open mind and find some resonance to the tune of my life.

Acknowledgements

Heartfelt gratitude to my guru, Sadhguru, and all the great masters who have walked upon this earth for offering the treasure of spirituality to me. Deeply grateful to my parents, family, relatives and my little sisters for your continued guidance and encouragement. Sincere thanks to my esteemed mentors and loving friends for your inspiration and solace. Deepest thanks to my husband and companion, Siddharth. Without your unwavering love and support, this work would not have been possible. My humble thanks to the nightly stars, nurturing earth and the life at large which opened ecstasies for me. Special thanks to my readers whose love for poetry make this journey worthwhile. Your support and appreciation are deeply valued.

Contents

Colours are borrowed
Even time leaves behind
Blissed
The moon stars with her golden gaze
Homecoming
Seeking
Burning
That run shall cease me
Playing in the waves of freedom
Devi
Devotion
Explosion
Mercy
Silence
Settled
Be

That Tomorrow

Standing by the window
On this calm, lonely night
My vision goes up-
Tiny stars hold my sight;
Shining so bright
In the dark, dark sky-
Tiny little dots, lighten my heart...
Like truths in a harmless little lie.
This night shall pass,
And the sun will rise
The morning will ease in
And a new day will arise.
The birds will chirp
The butterflies will fly
The trees will wake up
To vibrant hues in the sky.
The dew will dry up
The insects will graze,
Bees will set on a honey journey
Life will become a crazy chase.

The clouds will sail
And the ants will come in a queue
The squirrels will hurry
The nature will enjoy a day anew.

After a long, long day
The sun will set-
Day to Night
The moon is in wait.
So, here I stand
With a pen in my hand
Looking forward to that tomorrow,
Through my half open little window.

Spring

At rest, in the lap of nature
Am a witness
To this season's beautiful gesture!
So gorgeous is this transition- Spring!
Land and trees, all covered in green.
In a moment, the nature is bright;
The next, it hides in shade;
Again, gleams the sunlight;
Yet again it starts to fade.
Behold the trees gleefully swinging
Branches and leaves immersed in dancing;
Flowers are in full bloom
Driving away all vibes of gloom.
And when everything is still,
A soft cool breeze, I feel.
A crystal-clear sky, with lazy clouds-
Clouds both light and dark aloud;
Few little sparrows just chirping away
Oh! Such beauty is a spring day!

Starry Stories

An infinity of secrets
Waiting beneath the stars
They gently guard the golden truths
Wrapped within their transient hearts.

Each glowing dot like a seeking lover
Eternally searching for its beloved,
Tracing the same known path each night
With the same zest, refusing to fade.
In the depths of this dark universe
It has happily lost itself in its quest,
All lost lovers wrapped in the same darkness
As each flickering hope, reluctantly rest.

An infinity of secrets
Waiting beneath the stars
They may not be magical tales
But real bleeding scars.

Each silver dot once missed a silver lining
Each an unknown soul, a token of endurance,
Like a timid lamp still glowing so pure
Stuck and trapped in luminous candescence.
An embodiment of success studded with failure
Calling the fireflies to reach to them;
Themselves free from the toils of earth
Soothe the one that's still stuck in the same.

Must they wish to know themselves
As each twinkling dot becomes another:
The ocean pulls them away, twice from their self
Morning falsely promises to bring them closer.

Pleasant Day

On a calm pleasant morn
When the golden beams kiss my cheek
A mystic feel elates my heart
Rises in me, a warmth oblique.
I bend towards that dancing due
That plays to balance on the tip
Morning spreads its gentle touch
As into a drop this beauty slips.
With the buzz, the bees appear
They steal and add colour in the air
Softly alighting on cozy petals
In the flowers they begin their affair.
I behold this amazing nature
Each moment: a fulfilment of presence,
Love imparting a blushing glow
As deeper I indulge in its essence.
Wrapped in this envelope of love
I sit alone on a little patch of green
Love is rising all around
In me is contained a captured queen.

Words come Alive

When thoughts fly into my mind
And feelings brew in my heart,
Then if pen meets paper
Streams of words make their start.
Thoughts quarrel to appear first,
Words begin their worldly fight,
Feelings find its way between
Silently securing its mark tight.
Expressions reveal in diverse forms,
Some sweet, some dear, some forlorn,
Some wrapped in sense and meaning
Some in fragments, scattered and torn.
Precious thoughts of pearls
Cling to the strings of feel,
Smoothly gliding their flow
From the heart into the reel.
Joy leaps from within,
Pain craves its silent pattern,
Fear peeps rather slyly,
Solitude searches for companion.

Feelings enrich each thought
Thoughts magnify that feeling,
Words convey these emotions
In tender firm lettering.
In this game of mingling thoughts
To vast multitude of meaning,
To choose and pick perfect words
And in expressing their feeling,
I find a platform to lose myself
To find a new 'me' in me,
This is what makes it unique;
In ink and words, I find me free...

It is here

The hunger of happiness
The desire for peace
Drives us beyond mountains
Attracts people across seas.
We wait in impatience
For happiness to arrive;
But can not find it yet
So just keep hope in our strive.
We travel from slates to states
We push boundaries to countries,
And when possible, we wander
To planets and galaxies.
But where's the happiness?
Where's the peace?
Why in this search,
This patience does cease?
Something so simple
Why difficult to attain?
Because, the core of existence
Sadly, we have forgotten.

We forget to look at the sky
Under which we are living;
We forget to smell the earth
On which we are thriving;
We forget to feel the air
In which we are breathing;
We forget to admire our self
Which is the basis of our existing.
So, when we look deeper
To seek the truth of this absurdity
We may succeed in our search
For happiness, peace and tranquility!

Literature

Literature is an aspect of life
A profound way of expression;
It reveals one's concealed thoughts
And veiled feelings and emotions.
It's a flowing wave,
That for ever flows...
It's a silent tune,
That within our heart sings...
It's a gentle breeze,
That in our mind blows...
It is an appealing art,
Cultured age long since.

Literature was philosophy
Even before ancient ages,
When epics were composed
By Valmiki and Vyasdev sages.
Premchand and Panth
Had immense contribution,
Nirala and Verma

Are not to be forgotten.
Tennyson and Tagore
Did express so beautifully,
And words are scarce
For Shakespeare and Shelly.

Literature is all in expression
A game played by many-
Let it be great poets
Or simply You and Me!
The beauty of literature
Shall in every heart reside,
Its essence will ever be cherished
As long as men be alive...

Grandparents

*They are the legends
Of time, to us unseen;
With pure white hair
Their love is from within.
They are ancient
They are old
But precious are they,
A proof to old is gold.
They smell the past
They live the histories
They are endless oceans
Of fables and stories.
They have knowledge
Vast and immense
Their life is dense
With experience.
They are a serene
Wrapped in snow,
They are the one,
That make us glow.*

We are the childhood
That they endeared,
To keep us happy
They ever ensured.
So, in their memory
This poem shall succeed
To have such loving grandparents,
Is a blessing indeed!

Pussy cat

I wish, I were a pussy cat
With white coat of fur,
I could move around your house
And spend a few happy hour.
I would mew all day
And you would look at me;
Slowly would you take me home,
And your pet would I be.
When you give me rice and milk
I won't nag you for the fish,
But when you praise, "good kitty"
I would certainly go and lick the dish.
At times, I won't come to you
Hiding in a corner of your home
You'll call, "Kitty! Kitty! Where are you?"
Still won't reply to your curious tone.
Whole day, shall I play with you
Every sort of fun and game-
And when I do some wrong,
Don't you tell me- "Shame! Shame!"

When you leave for vacations
Thinking of all the joy and fun,
I would still wait all day,
In patience for your return.
I too would disappear for days,
Just a tease- a silly lie,
After every return, I would find you
And you would heave a breath of sigh.
With your loving hands,
On my back, will you pat...
I would close my eyes and purr,
"Thank God, I am your pussy cat."

Questions

I was sitting still
In the silence of time,
When queer questions flooded
In this prized mind of mine.
I want to know:
The true reality,
Who am I?
What is my identity?
What is my value?
What is my worth?
What is my meaning?
Why is my birth?
Why am I loved
By my parents and family?
What did you bring me for?
Am I free, really?
Why do I have,
This life as a gift?
Is there any relevance at all,
As to why I exist?

Searching

Solitude is sure sweet
When you yourself choose it,
But it's quite a bit bitter
When it is a thrusted gift.
In this solitude,
My heart feels restless.
It's threatening here,
I feel me become
Less and less.
I'm in search of an aspect,
Where I can pour --
Where it's not just me,
But so much more.
I want to be, one of the many;
But still, among all,
I want to be me.
Whoever I am,
Genuinely That I want to be,
I want to be myself-
And to be content with This me;

So, here I sit-
All confused and lost.
What's happening to me?
For what is this cost?
Where do I search,
For the missing me in my mind?
Why suddenly in me
Myself can't I find?

Noise of silence

Silence is –
When words don't speak
And ears don't hear
You might be holding my hand
Yet, I am nowhere near.
In some deep white serenity
You find yourself floating.
The brightness blinds you
At once you feel everything yet nothing.
You let it pain: tremendously;
Somewhere much deeper than your heart
Squeezing out last ounce of reason
And all that you mastered of life, in art.
This deafening silence
Kills you, every breath, from within
Only you know how splendid it feels
To forget all that your mind has seen.
And in ignorance is bliss
Repose: it pervades all dimension.
Nothing can match this placid silence

Which gently ends each emotion.
Silence grips you from within.
Silence envelopes you from without.
Suddenly the noise of silence is unbearable,
In silence, you silently shout.

In the mirror

Looking into the eyes
Of this girl in the mirror -
Finally, it dawns upon me,
Indeed, time has cost her dear.
With eyes drenched in pain
A face tired and morose
Lips stitched to prevent
Ordeals her heart endures,
Her eyes look into mine
Shadowing her heart, gripped in fear
Revealing the stark void in her soul
Speaking of being in terror smear.
She hopes for some hope
Through her helpless gaze
Then of a sudden
Her image turns haze.
I blink my eyes
Find tears on her cheek
Tears that roll alone
In the serene- meek and bleak.

The drops promise some hope
Endorsing the flame still lit
Though it's extremely dim
Yet, it didn't yet quit.
In some corner of her heart
I see her patience, in wait to bloom
This relieves my soul within,
The mirror finds a fading gloom.

It's my life

My Life is how I make it
Not what they say;
Life is walking along with me
Not stepping on every stone they lay.
My life is how I perceive it
And enjoy each and every moment,
It is how I own my happiness
Ever settled in peace and content.
For me, it's being brutally real
Looking forward and moving ahead,
Making along sweet memories
And adding hues that never fade.
It is in accepting the sorrow
Feeling that pleasure of pain,
And equally feel the surge to eternity
Standing in the blessed shower of rain.
Life is running into the lush green fields
Yet learning to keep me away from it,
Life is in cuddling my loved ones
Knowing, we might never again meet.

For me, life is a living
A living to the fullest of my extent:
It's just following my heart
Ensuring, I'm not condemned to repent.
Life is a journey of learning:
Of experiencing every moment
And spending some time with me
In introspecting to my content.
It is an enriching experience
Where no quest is worth my life,
It's an opportunity to grow myself
In each aspect of my strife.
Outcomes don't define my life,
It is only me who can decide;
And I am brave enough
To ride through this tireless tide.
It's me who has to live my life:
So, it's me who shall build it-
Failures are certain for sure
But that won't smudge my feat.
I have strength to stand up again
I have good reasons to lead, to live
I have hopes to raise my world
I have dreams I await to achieve.
I have a longing to live this life
Happily willing to heal my pain

And live with a fulfilled me
Through all the seasons of my terrain.

26

The seeming change

By the eternal law, times change.
Well, that is how it seems
Yet, nothing changes, not a thing
It's the same old story yet to begin...
Past becomes past.
And present is present.
No more does it last
That itself is the scent.
In this lives the reflection
Which is pushed aside,
But alas! Feelings are feelings
It drags you with its tide.
You scream, "no. No. NO."
Oh! Who does care?
It is beyond your fate.
It is beyond you to dare.
And yes, this is how it is.
This is how it has been through years.
This is how it will go on,
Gifting each their unfair share.

Farewell

Time and tide, Waits for none
Once it flows away, It is done.
However you complain,
How relentlessly you try,
But you are left rejected
Just to exhale a long deep sigh.
You cannot complain or scream,
Cause Nothing can avail to you
A 'time' that's now a dream.
You may long and dearly miss ,
Places and people- close to your heart
But you only shed silent tears
Since time is permitted to depart.
You can soothe yourself
By diving into the thoughts of past
But then it grows on you,
That those days no more do last.
The glorious golden times
That are now left to cherish,
You embrace them tight

And squeeze into sweet memories.
Your heart is full,
Yet your mind is blank
The journey so overwhelming,
Somehow, the destination shrank.
You feel elated and grateful,
For bundled years of momentful grace;
At least, "once upon a time—"
Brings a smile to your face.
So, you thank the almighty,
For this blessed gift-
Afterall, every ride to a peak
Also has a ride down from it.

To the society

All that you wanted me to be.
A 'grown up' right?
A (growth?) that's devoid me of?

I have lost my rhythm.
See, I am stuck in your chaos.
I have lost my ability to be happy.
True, to laugh out loud is gross.
I agree, life is no more a play.
I have turned dead serious.
I don't speak of my will;
If wrong, it may prove grievous.
I don't go about giggling anymore,
It's too insane in your sane society.
I cannot afford to be weak,
Or else I will be empathised with pity.
I must pretend to be strong,
If not, I am just too bad.
I must always wear a smile,
I know, it's shameful to be sad.

I should not touch the rain,
It's against the civilised way.
I should not walk barefoot,
The earth is dirty, you say.
The more I question my abilities
The more I cover with confidence;
To preserve my utter hollowness
Proudly I put up all defence;
I cannot retrieve to earn some rest,
Cause success is sold only to battles;
So, I build only prisons of fear
Cause grownups don't build castles.
I do miss my childhood.
I don't enjoy my present.
I seek solace in a false future,
Where being fake is the only content.
I proudly carry a long face.
A proof of maturity – being grave.
I display anxiety and stress,
And joy, for my coffin, I save.
I don't dare to question,
What if you can't answer?
I don't imagine any more.
What if dreams into reality transfer?
I must never follow my heart,
What if, I am wrong?
Here's no mercy for mistakes.

Instead, I was a mistake all along.

You dared me –
To try and not be a fail.
Now I dare you –
Just watch Onn
I will grow Beyond your scale.

Let me meet the end

It is the sharpest of all pain
It is deepest of all wound,
When I resolve to quit
Yet keep me bound.
The sweetness in my heart
Is now enveloped with thorns,
It does prick no more
But soothes the hollow groans.
The necklace of hope
Is scattered like stars
Just alluring pearls
Present in the endless darks.
No reason to move on
No destination to meet,
Why is this journey?
Who shall I greet?
Meaning has a meaning no more
Reason has lost every reason;
It's better to leave all behind
Than be in places turned prison.

I want to touch the end
I want to feel time stop.
I can stand it no more
To be trapped in a knot.
I refute my feelings
I refuse every defence,
Yet my heart holds me back
This resolute is not yet dense.
Here I am, holding the end
Yet cannot make love to it
Oh! How I wish I could strike,
To end it all in a beat.

Spark of the night

It's an immense feeling
As this gentle breeze blows
And along with it
The lonely tune of my heart flows...
Wherever I lay my eyes
It meets a dark immense
It's filled with emptiness
Its void full of fulfilled essence.
Millions of stars gaze at me
I stare only at one
All of them seem to know me
Yet, I know them none.
Scattered like shattered hopes
Tiny vestiges of lost precious dreams;
Still with a tint of longing
In their stare they seem to scream.
Clouds wander in the darkness
Hiding the stars from my stare
Its reminiscence strikes my being-
Reminding me, - I can dare.

Fantasy

Late night, a few hours to sunrise
In this silent house, everyone's asleep
Am the only one still awake...
Wondering- Why am I forbidden by sleep?
Staring at the immense heaven
Adored with embeddings of pearl
It seems, each one waits for someone
As this moonless night waits for her earl.
The trees breeze in subdued tune
Revealing glimpses of eloped blushing green
It tries to hide in its own shadow
The unmistakable tinge of a glowing sheen.
Softly passing the touch in its tone
This gentle breeze tinkles in the air
All the desires I wished to listen
Secretly, it whispers in my ear.
My heart brims full of love
I shut my eyes but they refuse to close
I wonder who has stolen my heart
For the one I am, I suppose.

Yet, something creeps deep in,
I look back into the dark:
All I find is a million dim lamps
Twinkling alone in the void stark.
I roll my eyes over the trees
The leaves, they droop in despair
Their dreams are mere dreams
Not a fragment of reality to share.
All that I wish to listen to,
In my heart, the air whispers
The pain of this duality
The mind never conquers.
Was it all just a fantasy?
All, that I had been weaving
Joining those sparkling diamonds
With emotions of love in my string.
Alas, reality hits hard reality
For fantasy, it has no space to spare
Indeed, fantasy is a falsity
Just a pleasing unreal affair.

Lost in love

If it were so, that I never met you!
Could I ever feel this pain?
The pain that ignites my heart
To love you again and again and yet again!
Even in my fancy, my fancies were false
But you proved it true; making me see –
Fancies are but shadows of the reality,
Here in your warmth, you envelope me.
When I try to find my true self,
I find me drenched in your affection,
Your love has seeped too deep
Through my bones, to this soul's connection.
I wonder, how you transformed it all!
As if, you yourself are the magical key:
Life – that resonates to mortality
You turned it into an eternity for me.
Tell me, how did you do this?
Why did you make me all yours?
The state that binds me now:
Is this the disease or the ultimate cure?

Colours are borrowed

She rests here in wait
Patient eyes – counting days roll in line
Steeped in her royal fragrance
She is the honeysuckle vine.
With her long tender tendrils
Through years she embraces the fence
A shadowy balcony houses her
She has grown with care dense.
Today, she is in full bloom
Youth has touched her green
White flowers adore her beauty
Indeed, she looks so serene!
None can miss her heavenly essence
With it, what can she win not?
The abundance of her sweet nectar
Makes her the queen of her sort.
She has a magical touch
Which can cure the ills
The fence knows it best
The witness to her skills.

It has seen kaleidoscope of butterflies
Come flapping their beautiful wings
The vine extends her plush green leaves
Gently they lay eggs- enclosing their offspring.
All the birds that happen to fly by
Are lost in praises of her pervading scent
But the honeysuckle secretly waits for her lover
The humming bird – for whom she is meant.
She knew, this spring he would visit her
The season of love kept her waiting
She could see her tiny lover
Coming along with his tuned humming.
He came flying in buzzing swirls
Forward he flied and backward drifted
He dropped from the top in a swift
Flied upside down in joy unlimited.
His gorgeous orange georgette neck
Refracted the sun and its blazing rays
In the magic of its bright feathers
The trapped honeysuckle gaped in maze.
She kept staring at her lover
With pollens full of dreams
She felt a bit ashamed of her plain beauty
In front of her lover's glowing beams.
He sucked from her flowers
He made her sweetness his own,
The honeysuckle blushed and glowed

They are the perfect lovers known.
She softly spread her divine fragrance
To envelope him with her dreamy touch
But how could he feel her essence
What is 'smell', he knew nothing as such.
Instead, all that he chirped
Made her stare blankly
Her long fairy-tale wait
Was not answered gently –
"Have you seen the sunflower
Such a perfect round as the sun
She lives only for the summer, true
But being with her is always fun.
With her big bright face
And soft pretty petals about
She is always so lively
For ever, she stands stout.
Her gifted golden glaze
Makes her the prettiest flower
You are beautiful too
But I wish you could be like her!"
A deaf silence followed...
She could not say much;
A gentle breeze caressed her wounded pride
She smiled at the old loving touch.
The fence gripped her firmly
She clutched to her ancient support

"Don't be disheartened my dear"
said the fence, "living is but a sport."
The dusky evening sky
Dewed her pure snowy petals
Spreading her fragrance to conquer the world
Within her a new realisation unfurls –
"How ignorant was I to wait for my love
Who can never let himself be mine,
He admits his love to the pretty sunflower
Yet, I would always prefer to be a honeysuckle vine."

Even time leaves behind

I embrace that loving touch,
I relish that moist imprint,
I relive this divine affection,
Everything, that has been bestowed since.
I shall eternally thank thee
For all that he blessed,
Gifted moments add essence,
My life keeps me amazed.
Memory adds to every moment
As pieces of time pass in a queue,
Their fragrance never fades,
Dear moments to cherish through.
Prized out fragments
Prove now all but priceless
Indeed, what a boon it is-
This heart in gratitude says.
This presence is sweet
Adding melody to the tune of life,
Yet, absence makes it sweeter
Adding hue to the reason to strive.

Absence tests my patience,
Patience enhances my eager;
Fleeting time shows the distance
Distance weaves, lost moments together.
In the tune that strings the stars,
In the fantasy the moon showers,
In the eternity the darkness envelops
In everything, I find an essence of hers.
Like the lonely moon in a silent night,
Like the fragrant earth on a drizzling eve,
Like the soothing breeze on a dreamy morn
Even time takes its virtuous leave.
It's difficult to bear the truth
Too painful to accept,
Yet there's hope to move on
For life says – "I move ahead".

Blissed

Who can love you more, than yourself?
Who can trust you, like you do?
Who understands you perfectly?
Who knows you best? Isn't it you?
You feel to the depth of your feelings;
You shed your pain with tears in a queue;
You listen to your heart in silent patience;
Who helps you heal? Isn't it you?

But believe me, you are not alone.
You never were,
You are caressed by the unknown.
There was always a morning
Where the sun does kiss;
There was never a night
Where the darkness do you miss;
There was for ever a day
Where the air does embrace;
But when did you cease to see
The nature that imparts you grace?

Where do you confide your secrets
On a dark raining eve?
With the dripping drops of sky
You let go of misery, as you grieve.
Where do you hide your fears
On the stormy nights of winters?
Then whom do you call
Isn't it the one, you seldom recall!
But she cares for you
Through all the times you smile and struggle;
You might forget to feel her presence
Yet you are swaddled safe in her cradle.

So, put down the weight,
Life is easy
Love your life
In "life" be busy.
Settle in your body,
See through your third eye
It will unveil the truth
You will shed the lie.
Love is all around
There's not a single scratch of hate.
This is not just magic
This is the only true state.

The moon stares with her golden glaze

The moon stares with her golden gaze
At the dark depths of the lake
Moonlight gently kisses her lover
Neither any absence nor abundance is fake.
A cool breeze blows and a question cripples
The water shivers into giggling ripples
Trees by the bank whisper in rustling leaves
The whole ambiance into enchantment steals.
Wrapped in the blissful sorrow
I adore the beauty, broad and narrow.
The sky is still yet its image is moving
So is life in thoughts and being.
The wavering image reflects:
A silent victory in each defeat;
Living alone in my solitude
I feel myself totally complete.

Homecoming

Back home- here am I, again.
Nothing has changed
Everything seems to be the same.
The same room. Same window.
But not the same view.
The trees are higher now
Covered in more lush green
I have grown up too
Life's become a monochrome film.
Same are these hot summer afternoons.
When a fierce cold wind gushes in
The curtains flutter like fire
Unsettled, this soul, sits silent within.
It starts to rain;
Behold: the smell hasn't changed,
Drenched petrichor is same as any bit.
The dreamy romance of such rain:
Now I dare say, I have lived through it.
The drizzle turns to shower
And the thundering is high

I would've cried like years earlier
But no, grownups don't cry.
Mom and dad: scolds and cuddles,
The air in my home
And their love has not changed
Instead, a strange distance has grown.
Today, something am I
Something else, I wanted to be,
A visit to home showed me all,
Of a past me.

Seeking

It's a strange feeling
That surges in my heart,
A deep sense of insecurity
That tries to tear me apart.
Why in this divine bliss
Immense untold pain accompany?
Why the more emotions bloom
More squeezes this heart in agony?
Days to be smeared with happiness
Find only rare speckles of joy,
This soul helplessly shrieks in pain
As the eternity, sorrow seems to destroy,
Doubts envelop undoubting virtues
Reality shatters reality;
Undying faith appears transient,
Unfailing belief seems to fade slowly.
Where days are coloured fantasy
And nights are dark mares,
Happiness and sorrow strive alone,
No more they form a pair.

Something stings my heart
Something breaks my peace
But what is this something
That I really need to seize?
I want an answer
An insight to gain,
I want to know
What's making me insane!
Nothing is stable, not a thing
No balance of mind,
No steadiness of being;
Something deep is changing,
Something that I can't find point,
Everything is churning
As if... I am disappearing.

Burning

All of it shalt be burnt-
All that's of me,
But not me.

Heaps and heaps of felt emotions
Squeezed in the corners of the yellow pages
From ages of my younger days
When paper gave shelter to this refugee,
The creations of growing years through art
In bright colours and black ink
The left overs in which my past days live,
All of it, into oblivion must sink.
All of it shalt be burnt-
All that's Of me,
But not me.

The threads of bound and knot relations
Worldly commitments of love, hatred, duty,
People who nurtured me up
People who were nurtured by me

Enemies to whom ego has sworn
Lovers for whom love was trapped,
Duties entangled with decades of emotion
All these strings that touch me, must be snapped.
All of it shalt be burnt-
Cause all this is Of me,
But not me.

This flesh and blood in beauty and youth
That fools every man and its master too
That which is acquired since moment first
The careful crafts of nature in years through,
This body that craves for the touch of lust
And withers in the lushful drought it suffers
Deep brown eyes, round nose, soft lips,
All of this body, back to earth, must be offered.
All of it shalt be burnt-
Cause all this is Of me
But not me.

All of it must be burnt
That is Of me
But NOT me.

That run shall cease me

I wish to snap all bond
Break every clutch through
And then run a wild
Into the envelope of virtue.
No care shall hold me bondage
No thread to pull my heart
No love to impress me with
No praise to smudge my art.
I'll run and run and run
Run through the endless miles I can't see
I'll run into a world unknown
Where I need to pay no kind of fee.

No bait shall snatch my glance
No emotion shall weaken my pace
No fear shall grip my heart
No danger shall win my gaze
No cause will dare to be
No reason shall try to reason
No faith shall raise hope

No meaning shall try to define.
I'll run and run and run
Run through the endless miles I can't see
I'll run into a world unknown
Where I need to pay no kind of fee.

I won't pause and run at stretch
Will run faster than I can
Just run aimed at the void
Defying all norms and ban.
I'll run through the night's darkness
I'll run in the sun's shine
I'll run through the shower's drizzle
This run will just be mine.
I'll run and run and run
Run through the endless miles I can't see
I'll run into a world unknown
Where I need to pay no kind of fee.

I won't cease this run
Yet, this run shall cease me-
There, where the sea ceases the sky
And the sky ceases the sea.
I will fade in that virtue
Ever enveloped in eternity
Then, when I be raised again
No longer shall I be with me.

Playing in the waves of freedom

Standing by the shore
For endless years long;
I listened patiently
To the sea's solitary song.
Waves would rise
Rush and fall at my feet,
Initially, it didn't touch
With time, they gently did.
That touch of freedom
Pervaded my heart
I waited for the tallest wave
To dash me apart.
I looked across the horizon
With eyes full of hope;
The cool breeze soothed my soul
Patience helped to cope.
In that monotonous rule
At last, stirred a change:
A giant wave came rushing

Awaiting an amazing exchange!
The huge wave crashed on me
Pulled me off with its flow
I lost to the immense-
Still, I admired its glow.
Beneath that wonder
I found wonders more
There was happiness,
Bliss fulfilling to the core;
Lost in that world,
I didn't search for me
I just loved my self
I denied to sea.
Still up my eyes rolled
Through that filter new:
The sky was different now
Yet it was blue.
Receded the wave,
Shivering am I
The same breeze blows
But frozen I lie.
That wait has faded
Instead, a challenge won-
It's to play a better game
In the waves dashing and gone.

Devi

She never gave birth to my soul
But she has relentlessly set me free
Before witnessing the silver lining
A vision of hers was all I did see.
She never looked after my feelings
But my seeking was nurtured my her,
She never cared for my emotions
But she kept my faith, with gentle care.
I thought she never heard my plea
But she always shed a tear in my pain;
She was never willing to teach me lessons
Just urging me to lose it all, and live again.
She was here, even before my call
She would never leave me helpless,
And I could never find me without her-
She embraced me into her ocean of grace!

Devotion

What are words, when
You are burning,
Burning with ecstacy—
How do I care for me?
How do I not care for me or you?
Who I am— It is You!
Just You – and You – and You.
Where to begin?
Where to pause?
Where to end?
Where to be?
— When I am everywhere – with You
In each piece of You – I be.

Explosion

This life's so fragile
Yet its experience so profound-
There's explosion of emotions
That knows no bound.
I guess, that's the clue
That this life is boundless?
It's not in days and years
But in moments we express.
So, whatever's fair and unfair
Just soak in the experience:
Live it to be free and full;
Don't mess to make it sense.
It is in its intensity
That this ride becomes interesting
It all comes to a certain end
Without meaning to becoming.
Let not a bit of me be saved
In this tremendous implosion;
I am willing to lose it all
Be consumed in life's explosion!

Mercy

Oh my Guru,
How do I speak of thee?
You opened your heart to me-
While I couldn't let me be mine;
I don't even deserve a speck of dust
And you bestowed me, the Divine!

Though I suffered in pain,
In unconscious ignorance
Yet it's insignificant,
Not worth your embrace;
But your compassion, O Divine master!
You soaked me in your overflowing grace.

Not knowing what to ask for,
I bowed for all I have
I couldn't recognise your love
You crave to give with such ease
But I am still so poor,
I am not able to receive.

All that this 'I' can do—
Meekly seek to merge in you:
So, with folded hands,
I ask for thee?
With your open arms
You offer me mercy!

Silence

This silence- so deep
It exists beneath any depth;
This silence- so pitched
It extends beyond bandwidth;
This silence- so loud
It can deafen a crowd;
This silence- so still
No movement can kill;
This silence- is exuberance
In it I can abandon in dance;
This silence- so consuming
In it I can dissolve my being;
Yet this silence- so liberating
Released to iterate
That I am no being!

Settled

Words are profusely uttered
Without a vibration;
Actions are actively performed
Without an impression;
Thoughts are swirling about
Without a ripple;
Desires are showing up
Without a riddle;
Emotions are playing out
Without a veil;
Living life in an intensity so high:
Everything's Here, without a trail.

Be

These eyes are not to see
But to calmly close;
These ears are not to hear
But to know the silence;
This mind is not to think
But to drive my being;
This heart is not to love
But to sustain the flame;
This body is not to treat
But a tool to be free;
This breath is not to flutter
But to be stunning still;
This life is not a gift
But a path to the truth;
And this me is not to be,
But to become:
That which is not me.

www.ingramcontent.com/pod-product-compliance
Lightning Source LLC
Chambersburg PA
CBHW061707130726
47996CB00006B/2203